OUR WOODLAND BIRDS

OUR WOODLAND BIRDS

A NATURE LOVER'S GUIDE

MATT SEWELL

EBURY
PRESS

1 3 5 7 9 10 8 6 4 2

Published in 2014 by Ebury Press, an imprint of Ebury Publishing

A Random House Group Company

Copyright © Matt Sewell 2014

Matt Sewell has asserted his right to be identified as the author of this Work in
accordance with the Copyright, Designs and Patents Act 1988

The Random House Group Limited Reg. No. 954009

Addresses for companies within the Random House Group can be found at
www.randomhouse.co.uk

A CIP catalogue record for this book is available from the British Library

The Random House Group Limited supports The Forest Stewardship Council®
(FSC®), the leading international forest-certification organisation. Our books
carrying the FSC label are printed on FSC® -certified paper. FSC is the only
forest-certification scheme supported by the leading environmental organisations,
including Greenpeace. Our paper procurement policy can be found at
www.randomhouse.co.uk/environment

To buy books by your favourite authors and register
for offers visit www.randomhouse.co.uk

Design by Two Associates
Colour reproduction by Altaimage
Printed and bound in China by Toppan Leefung

ISBN 9780091957902

For my goldfinches, Jess and Romy and Mae

CONTENTS

FOREWORD

Matt is an illustrator whose drawings I love
to look at. Here's why. They are beautifully
drawn and painted. Matt's style is his own,
totally, but it reminds me of a favourite of
mine, Edward Lear, funny and affectionate
towards the birds. The design of his books,
harks back to bird books I pored over when
I was a boy. The drawings, while they are
Matt's style, are correct. Colours and shape,
it's important! Like his other books, Our
Garden Birds and Our Songbirds, this is Our
Woodland Birds. British Birds, you see. They
are Matt's passion, and mine. Because they are
with us all the time. Have a look, in the city,
in the countryside, at the seaside, they are our
companions. Matt draws the birds like that.

Edwyn Collins, February 2014

INTRODUCTION

You can learn more from a thirty-minute walk through the woods than you could from a whole day of watching television. Forests of pine, oak and beech all have their own individual vibes and inhabitants, and every tree is an intricate ecosystem providing food, shelter and playgrounds to animals of every shape and size. Many of our favourite birds have adapted to thrive in this environment whatever the season, and it is an absolute joy to ramble with them in their natural habitat. Birds love the woods even more than we do.

THE BIRDS

A Charm of Goldfinches
in a Common Ash
Carduelis carduelis

With mercurial giggles like the tinkling of tiny bells, it's easier to hear a charm of Goldfinches than to see one when you're in the woods. These forest dwellers can be heard and spotted anywhere, from dense forestation, gardens and parks, to busy town streets. Like a caravan of golden lucky charms bouncing and chortling their way to the next port of call, be that feeder, thistle or forest.

Mr & Mrs Bullfinch
in a Common Pear Tree
Pyrrhula pyrrhula

The crimson squire and his desaturated but no-less stunning wife gently move through the forest in unison, as bright and soft as the fruits of the buds they eat. So handsome and unassuming, they are like a successful, attractive couple who have moved to the countryside to raise their even more beautiful children safely in a woodland idyll. Living the dream, they sing to each other as they go – their vocabulary has no alarms or threats, just that simple mellow song.

Crested Tit
in a Scots Pine
Lophophanes cristatus

As tits go, the crested ones are the jewels in
the feathery crown, not just because of their
immaculately coiffured reverse quiffs, but also
because on our islands they are found only in
the isolated, frozen reaches of the northern
pine forests of Scotland. The people who live
in this dramatic, awesome landscape will be
well acquainted with them, as they stop off
at the bird feeders to have a break from their
usual pine seeds. Those lucky, lucky people.

A Winter's Tangle of Tits

When the cruel jaws of winter are clenched
tight, the forest can appear to be a crystal
cavern suspended in a moment of time, when
the moon is forever full and the air is a hung,
sparkling mist. Its denizens are hopefully
hidden and dreaming the winter away. But
spirits do glow in these cold times, chirping
and tweeting through the frosty mist and ice
needles. Firecrests, Goldcrests and tits of all
kinds drift as one and puff like warm pockets
of air through the wintry wildwoods in
search of food and shelter, thawing
the ice and souls as they go.

Long-tailed Tit
in a Hawthorn Tree
Aegithalos caudatus

Hidden away deep in the heart of sharpness, the
spiky interior of a spiteful hawthorn tree, lies
the unlikely and inhospitable home of one of
nature's most pleasant of fellows – the Long-
tailed Tit. Protected by a chaos of tiny spears,
ensconced and safe from harm, this mossy
cave is a work of perplexing wonderment.
Containing thousands of feathers, tiny clumps
of moss and tender lichen, the nest is woven
together dexterously with wool and spiders'
webs. Nest-building for Long-tailers is an
activity for the whole family, as previous broods
and extended kindred all chip in with the
material collecting and building. Amazingly,
they also help feed and raise the young as the
enchanting nest stretches with every new brood.

Hobby
Falco subbuteo

———

At the skirt of an immense primeval forest
resides a tiny falcon with striking markings
and fantastic colours. The Hobby's
gentlemanly navy blue is contradicted
delightfully with a pair of scraggy red surf
shorts, resembling a stowaway admiral,
if such a thing can be imagined.

Fans of pre-historic/pre-computer football-
related pastimes might notice something
familiar about his Latin name. The inventor of
the massively popular post-war football game
Subbuteo originally tried to trademark the
game's name as the prosaic and rather boring
'Hobby'. Luckily, failing to do so, he took
inspiration from the magnificent Hobby
and created a wonderful moniker.
An inspiring bird in many ways!

Merlin
Falco columbarius

This rustic falcon can easily be confused with
another rufous raptor, the Kestrel. They share
a big-eyed feline appearance, shape, colour and
size, although in the air our Merlin has more
of a rudimentary hang compared to that of the
Kestrel's heavenly hover. Once you can tell the
difference, the Merlin is an amazing bird to
spot, so sit back and enjoy our smallest bird of
prey. He may not be a magician, but he is most
definitely a very competent wonder worker.

Common Buzzard
Buteo buteo

A great place from which to spot the Buzzard is simply out of the car window, as he perches high in a tree on the side of the road, watching his kingdom fly by. Our tiny eagle, blonde patchy and compact, he can always be found soaring upon high-raising warm waves above farmlands, rolling hills and old oak forests. A distant sabre-rattling cry of 'Peejay!' lets you know exactly who is up there in the clouds and who is running the show.

Goshawk
Accipiter gentilis

When our fields and towns were all just one big swathe of trees, the Goshawk would have inhabited these lands in great numbers. A big bird that can take big prey – in the past maybe geese to derive its name, but these days their fearsome talons fall upon other woodland-dwelling birds, in particular the Pheasant. This great hawk's taste for game has unfortunately led it into the crosshairs of gamekeepers, who will do anything to protect their hunt and who have persecuted the Goshawk to such low numbers that they had to be reintroduced. Leaving aside the politics of Pheasants, the Goshawks have a grand old time come spring when they take to the air, performing sky-dances above the trees. Goshawks plunging from great heights to rise romantically in unison is one of the forest's many signifiers of the turning of the seasons.

Sparrowhawk
Accipiter nisus

Pray you do not catch the evil eye of the female Sparrowhawk – the fiercest hunter in the woods. She's twice the size of the male, with her haunched twin engines that burst through the looming leaves like a medieval laser. Any bird is a sitting duck and can be effortlessly plucked from its perch and thrown to the ground where it will be coldly clasped, writhing, shrouded with an impenetrable wall of steely feathers. It's not just Sparrows she's after: Blackbirds, Wood Pigeons and even young Sparrowhawks are all on the menu. No wonder birds always look so nervous when this lady is around.

The Nuthatch and the Treecreeper
Sitta europaea and *Certhia familiaris*

These guys have a lot going for them; not only are they lucky enough to be able to fly, it's their second nature to walk wherever they want to, paying little regard to the lesser laws of science such as gravity and things like that. Both are committed forest dwellers and can be confused when they are racing around tree trunks, so here is a cunning phrase to help you tell the difference: hatches go up, trees come down.

It is largely believed that the Treecreeper is the only British bird able to walk down trees. Having said that, the Nuthatch has enough bravado and bluster that he can do whatever he wants, whenever he wants and nobody is going to stop him.

Wryneck
Jynx torquilla

The Wryneck is quite queer, a woodpecker from the old world, a bird of witchcraft that was used for casting spells, hexes and jinxes – see his Latin moniker. With a marbled camouflage designed for the forest floor, it feeds almost exclusively upon ants amongst the decaying bark and leaves. The deck is not the safest place for a small bird such as the Wryneck, so in their defence they writhe their necks to disturbing angles and hiss like snakes, hence the name and their association with the unearthly. Creepy.

Lesser Spotted Woodpecker
in a Cherry Plum Tree
Picoides minor

An easy way to tell the difference between
this and the Greater Spotted Woodpecker
is that this fellow is tiny – only the size of a
Great Tit. The Greater Woodpecker is nearly
twice the size, and twice as common. Both
have the distinct mottled dazzling black and
white climbingwear and red fascinators. The
Lesser Spotted's headwear is distinguishable, as
though wearing a beret, and they are of a much
more gentle nature altogether, possessing none
of the bullish ladisms of the other woodpeckers.
Preferring to keep itself to itself, the Lesser
Spotted Woodpecker hides away in the outer
reaches and copses of our forests.

A Flight of Finches

Birds of a feather flock together and, when
it gets cold, they endeavour together as well.
Feeding, resting and having fun is dangerous
after the leaves have fallen and there are
Sparrowhawks about. Safety in numbers is the
wisdom of birds, as finches of all shapes and
sizes, including Bramblings and lovely little
Siskins, gather on the forest floor, excitedly
foraging and feeding where the seeds
of the forest gather.

So on some frosty ramble through your local
hinterland, do not be dismayed if you struggle
to identify what type of gregarious bird is
banqueting a stone's throw away, as it might
be a charm of every single finch ever invented.

Pheasant
Phasianus colchicus

Along with roads, public libraries and stinging nettles, the Pheasant was one of many wonderful things that the Romans brought to Britain. So don't listen to the nonsense put forward by certain members of society who claim that the Pheasant was introduced only for sport – he has been dashing from the undergrowth and over roads long before the gun was even invented. Bottle green and glorious golden chestnut, with a long tail that streaks like a comet, the Pheasant is a work of celestial beauty.

Golden Pheasant
Chrysolophus pictus

Like a mythical Mayan sunburst god, the
Golden Pheasant has somehow found a home
in our green and damp lands. I am lucky
enough to have spotted one in the wild,
even though I have to admit, I thought I was
hallucinating at the time. This must be the
perpetual effect these quixotic creatures have
on any beholder lucky enough to stumble
upon these astral projections whilst
rambling through the woods.

Black Grouse
Tetrao tetrix

Hidden amongst scattered birch in boggy, cold places or running amok in conifer plantations, the boreal pine ladykiller struts his stuff. The Black Grouse looks good and he knows it. He is the peacock of the north with his fan-like tail and intense display, and the ladies just swoon. In springtime, great processions of Black Grouse meet at their annual 'lek' in clearings within the forest. The males dance, fight and sing to impress the hens, whilst the victorious alpha-Grouse makes off with a bevy of wives for his hillside harem. Sounds like a great night out. Here's hoping their numbers increase soon.

Goldeneye
Bucephala clangula

This gorgeous duck is a recent introduction
to these islands, previously just passaging
and taking winter countryside holidays here.
They've stayed thanks to specially designed
Goldeneye nest boxes that line the banks of
their favourite lakes. So now these fowls have
no need to uproot and migrate; they
can stay here all year round.

Moorhen
Gallinula chloropus

As names go they haven't really got this one right, as this guy is obviously of the *Gallinula* genus rather than the *Gallus* of the chicken, obviously. And another thing, the Moorhen is found everywhere from urban parks to woodland ponds, but not really up on the moors. Weird.

Woodcock
Scolopax rusticola

A wader of leaves rather than tides. Hidden
amongst fallen forest flotsam and jetsam,
moth-like it sits, sloth-like it moves under the
stippled light of the moon. With his coat of
many dull colours, the Woodcock is almost
an impossible spot, so put the binoculars
away and keep an ear out, for the best way to
observe these stumpy plumpers is by listening
at night to their low-slung, airy croak. Like the
birds themselves, the Woodcock's lovesong
is a curious and glorious thing.

Serin
in a Douglas Fir
Carduelis spinus

With their verdant and tawny colouring, it's easy to confuse the sweet Serin with the larger and more popular Greenfinch, Siskin or even Yellowhammer. So just look for a camouflaged canary that's gone camping and you'll soon be able to tell the difference. Easy.

Whinchat
Saxicola rubetra

Like his cousin the Stonechat, this handsome
gent is heard rather than seen. Preferring the
safety of tree plantations and tall grass, the
Whinchat bounces to perch upon stumps and
fenceposts to chatter as loud as he can. Very
nervous when out in the open, he is gone
before you know it, giving you no chance to
gaze upon his great orange and brown
colour combination. So listen with
your eyes next time.

Cirl Bunting
in a Crack Willow
Emberiza cirlus

Sage green, butter yellow and earthy ochre are
the colours daubed upon this rare Bunting
who, without the details, could easily be
mistaken for a Yellowhammer. Just as bright
and breezy a bird, but it's an altogether
different story when it comes to population;
the Yellowhammer is native to thousands of
glades, tracks and fields the length and breadth
of the country, whilst our Cirl Bunting is
confined to just a pocketful in coastal Devon.
For what was once a commonplace bird
across southern Britain, their severe drop in
numbers caused concern. Great work is being
done down there to help the Cirl community
grow and to create an understanding of what
happened to prevent a repeat in the future.

Woodlark
Lullula arborea

This stocky, streaked songbird likes nothing more than to sing his song all day long, whether he is hidden in a tree or cascading through the air, circling and reciting his song cycles for everyone in auditorial range. The larks are kings of audacious vocalisation and well and truly deserve the subtle feathered crowns that adorn them.

Tree Pipit
in a Maritime Pine
Anthus trivialis

The Tree Pipit is just one of many birds that arrive for summer after a long journey from a winter in Africa, bringing their songs, zest and commotion with them, warming the earth and our hearts as they go.

Bluethroat
in a Birch Tree
Luscinia svecica

No, your eyes do not deceive you! Such a bird
does exist and pops over from Europe and
northern Africa on the early summer breeze,
looking not too dissimilar to a Robin that's
gone wild in his mum's make-up bag when her
back was turned. If you spot a Bluethroat give
yourself a high five and the nearest person a
cuddle, as you have done very, very well.

Black Redstart
in a London Plane Tree
Phoenicurus ochruros

Cousin to the woodland-dwelling Redstart, the Black Redstart has chosen to spread his wings and branch out from the rocky forest edge, taking up roost in the city. Getting a job as a chimney sweep and a bijou apartment in the heart of the city, this metropolitan Redstart is an amazing spot for any urban bird lover. Long may the adventure continue.

Ring Ouzel
in a Dogwood Tree
Turdus torquatus

This dapper Blackbird's brother is just as much a thrush as a Robin or Nightingale; a thrush doesn't just wear a spotty vest – sometimes it can wear a dinner jacket too. The Ouzel is more commonly spotted in scattered trees on scrubby hillside, but he must have made a few visits into town as his look has caught on with the fashionable urban Blackbirds as they try to mimic his dashing neck ring with their bleached albino patches. They just never get it quite right though, do they?

Fieldfare
in a Common Yew
Turdus pilaris

I always thought Fieldfares were a bit boring,
a bit middle of the road in their sensible grey
and brown attire, but after considering how far
they fly to visit us every year they are anything
but. Along with many other birds, they set
sail on cold westerly winds from Scandinavia
and come and stay with us for winter, feasting
on every bright red berry going, such as
holly, rowan and yew. Everything except the
red fleshy berry on a yew tree is poisonous,
including the pip. Lots of birds including
the Fieldfare know this and use the yew as a
regular stop off for winter nutrition. A super
food for the super starved after a
long flight from abroad.

Waxwings
in a Rowan Tree
Bombycilla garrulus

The colder the winter, the bigger the irruption
of Waxwings. Westward they fly from
northern Europe in search of less treacherous
temperatures and food, lots of food. Britain
offers many a seasonal bountiful feast for
many a weary traveller – juniper, mistletoe
and rowan berries are favourites amongst
those circles, and for Waxwings in particular,
who also have a taste for crabapples and can
decimate an orchard in mere minutes, gorging
themselves, panic eating, berry binge drinking.
Stuffing themselves to capacity. Often the
Waxwings have been observed passing berries
to each other before consumption, forming
bonds and strengthening friendships
before the long journey home.

Spotted Flycatcher
in a Hazel Tree
Muscicapa striata

From his perched vantage point, the Spotted Flycatcher leaps, somersaults, dives and twists to catch not only flies but moths, beetles, butterflies and even those horrible summer wasps that try to ruin your picnic. They may be a bit dull looking but they do everything with heart and are really anything but.

A Parliament of Young Tawny Owls
Strix aluco

Beyond the tall beech and the thick oak carpet lies a heavily guarded secret. In a well-hidden location deep within the glades is the habitat of the Tawny Owl and its family. After nesting in an obscured tree-hole, the den eventually gets too small for the fluffy owlets, who spill out and perch close by with their already developed strong talons. They squat patiently, awaiting feeding with large eyes as dark as a raven and their wisping, downy feathers as soft as a moth's eyelash. Such a pretty sight comes with a cost: the fledglings are protected viciously by their parents night and day – the silent killers of the forest.

European Eagle Owl
Bubo bubo

Many thousands of years have passed since this
mighty Eagle Owl was a *bona fide* resident
of the British Isles; now a very small number
are back by means unknown, but it's a vastly
different place since they were last here. A
huge owl and viciously territorial, he won't
suffer any fools, hawks or harriers, never
mind any other owls nearby. No doubt they
are a glorious and extravagant edition to our
landscape, but a cautious orange eye is being
kept upon them as a thousand years could pass
and the European Eagle Owl with his capitalist
tactics could be the last one standing.

Great Grey Shrike
in a Blackthorn Tree
Lanius excubitor

The wanna-be raptor who wears a mask to
conceal his identity amongst his fellow birds.
Perched up high he surveys his plot before
dropping down on his prey, be it mammal,
insect or another bird. They then preserve
their quarry impaled on the barbarous barbs
of a blackthorn bush; this is their larder and
this is what gives all shrikes the gruesome
sobriquet of The Butcher Bird!

Red-backed Shrike
in a Hawthorn Tree
Lanius collurio

With conker-red wings, club-like beak and a long tail that disguises the fact that they are not much bigger than a House Sparrow – so smaller than their cousin, the Great Grey Shrike, but every bit as hawk-like and brutal. Their skewered mammal kebab shops have given shrikes a bad name – in fact in Germany they were called The Destroying Angel. Wow, that certainly is a bad name for somebody who is a very welcome visitor. Just don't tell the local animal population that they're coming.

Jay
in an English Oak
Garrulus glandarius

One of the moustachioed Jay's favourite foods, apart from woodland delicacies such as bugs and brambles, is the mighty acorn. He frantically collects them, hiding them all around his patch. Many are forgotten and eventually germinate and become the forest's new saplings rather than a hungry crow's stored lunch.

The English oak is a wondrous tree, held sacred in ancient times and now worshipped by woodland walkers. Its wood has been utilised in everything from man's earliest tools to his biggest of ships. But disregarding our endeavours, it is for nature that the oak is the highest prize. A constant giver of food and protection throughout every season for every conceivable soul in the forest. Outliving us by many hundreds of years, each oak tree is a world in itself with roots that run deep.

Nutcracker
in a Stone Pine
Nucifraga caryocatactes

A Siberian starling, but very much of the
crow family, comes dressed in the finest dark
hues of an autumn/winter range and dazzling
snowflake parka jacket. An infrequent winter
visitor from northern Europe, the Nutcracker
gets his name from his love of . . . can you
guess? Yes, cracking nuts! Using his long
beak to chisel out pine seeds all winter long, a
cracker – like the Jay – systematically buries
and stores their chow to keep for refreshments
at less plentiful times; they have been known to
store up to 30,000 seeds in one season.
That's a lotta nuts cracked!

Jackdaw
Corvus Monedula

As crows go, the Jackdaw is only small, so that makes them ideal for squeezing into small places – they love to nest in tree-holes and other nooks and crannies hidden away in the woods. This agoraphobic tendency also means that they love to nest in ill-chosen places too, such as chimney pots, which can lead to calamitous and farcical situations. Take it from me, a soot-covered Jackdaw flying round your house is a very startling thing to encounter.

A Rookery
Corvus frugilegus

Long before the dandelions have popped or
the crocuses have crocked, the Rook is the
industrious early bird in the late winter frost.
Way up in the nooks of outer branches of
high climbing trees such as the beech, ash
and sycamore, the barefaced crows build
their bulbous twiggy homes. Despite their
oily, ominous appearance, they are the least
sinister of the crows and are in fact extremely
sociable. Their high-rise canopy communes
are as thriving and bustling as any market
thoroughfare and just as noisy. Though
sometimes too noisy, and with the Rook not
being a protected bird, the odd cull has been
known to take place when their township
is bursting at the seams.

Hooded Crow
Corvus cornix

A welcome addition to the *Corvus* genus from north of the border. This Scottish crow is almost exactly the same as our crow apart from the grey rollneck tank top which is used as an extra layer to help keep them warm against the driving wind and rain. They don't have quite as much of the loner attitude as the Carrion Crow, although they are still up for a bit of skulking, stalking and sulking. They can be seen at times with wider social circles, hanging out and loitering like disenfranchised youths with other hoodies before they start getting back into bother again.

A Tidings of Magpies
Pica pica

. . . Three for a girl, Four for a boy . . . What
do you get for five . . . ? Hang about, what
do you get for a whole treeful? I remember
being truly spooked at seeing anything over
a single magpie when I was a kid; I'd run and
hide like I'd just seen the hoof prints of the
Devil himself. With little disregard to over-
imaginative children, a tidings of Magpies
is generally formed during the winter, when
families join together in a colossal, bald tree
where they gather with intent and
hatch wicked deeds.

Bramble-picking Blue Tits
Aprus caeruleus

I've always loved fruit crumble, tarts and breaking the seal of a glistening jar of home-made jam bursting with dark berries, each lovingly picked with cold, sore hands and placed in an old ice cream tub. But those blackberries and raspberries weren't put there just for us to enjoy! The bird world has been bramble-picking long before we knew how to bake. These scratchy bushes flower their fruit with only birds in mind. Popular chaps such as the Blue Tit and Blackbird love a good juicy berry and will feed to their heart's content before flying off and plopping the seeds out the other end, helping the thorny bushes to advance their spiked grip of occupation of the forest floor, where space is at a premium. Blackberry bushes are masters of this sharp strategy, but as the Blue Tits know, those berries makes it all a little bit sweeter.

Redpoll
in an Alder Tree
Carduelis flammea

A pretty, native bird who looks like an
autumnal Linnet that's feeling the cold and got
her winter woolies out. A bright, sociable finch
with a small beak for picking the tiniest of
seeds, the Redpoll hangs out in large
flocks and chuckles as it flies.

Golden Oriole
in a Cornelian Cherry Tree
Oriolus oriolus

A rare but annual summer visitor from Europe
that, considering their vivid glow, is tricky to
spot once it is up amongst the canopy leaves
where it prefers to reside. You may only know
of the Oriole's presence by the floaty pan-
piped song that drifts down from the frond,
bringing a touch of the exotic with it to the
lucky forest chosen by these dazzling
but bashful birds.

Ring-necked Parakeet
in a Beech Tree
Psittacula krameri

Legend has it that Jimi Hendrix released a
flock of Parakeets to liven up a dull London
sky in the swinging sixties. However they
got here they have certainly brought some
groovy colours and far-out vibes to London's
heaths, commons, parks, and everywhere else
in between. Although they haven't gone down
too well with the locals, as the Parakeets bully
indigenous birds away from their patches and
eat all the grub. So it's hard to tell if they get
their names from their jazzy markings or
because you want to wring their necks.

Stock Dove
Columba oenas

You know how every now and then you see a pigeon that's much nicer than your normal feral pigeons? You're taken aback by its pretty face, softly hued shades and its lovely, kind demeanour – it's not begging or hassling, just going about its business. Well, I can bet any money that pigeon was actually a Stock Dove. So we really should be nicer to the rats-with-wings type of pigeons as they are descended from the Stock Dove, their amiable pastel ancestor.

Blackcaps
and Mistletoe
Sylvia atricapilla

Maybe not a warbler by name, but he is so in form, function and voice. A sleek, handsome bird, male becapped in black and the lady in chestnut red. A favoured sustenance for these European winter visitors that alight here is the otherworldly mistletoe. Not just for snogging under, the mistletoe has been revered since the days of the Druids, who would cut the magical white berries with a golden sickle for sacrifices, rituals and divination. Its enchanting influence probably derives from the fact that the plant is a parasitic shrub that would conjure itself out of the ether. Maybe the Druids hadn't noticed that after eating the berries the Blackcaps would fly to other trees and wipe their messy beaks covered in sticky mistletoe seeds on to the fresh branches, providing new ground for the mystical wandering weed. Magic!

A Siege of Herons
Ardea cinerea

He may have the air and mystique of the lone
fisherman battling the elements to snatch a
tiny fish from the brackish waters, sadly flying
solo except for the maddening, mobbing
crowd of crows who follow his every move,
continually mistaking him for a Golden Eagle,
but the truth is that the Heron is far from
being lonesome. He lives in a communal roost
with his fellow fisherfriends, high in the trees
on the water's edge, swaying in their nests,
scruffy, twiggy and flat like a makeshift raft.
The heronry, with up to six or seven nests per
tree, is a busy and bustling place; no wonder
the Heron prefers to spend his days away from
home, fishing and taking in the serenity
of the countryside.

Barn Owl Nest Box
Tyto alba

With its heart-shaped face and feathers of the purest white that shine through the gloaming, the Barn Owl is easily one of the most beautiful owls in the plethora that the world has to offer. Traditionally a resident of barns and other sheltered places, a perfect habitat is not always easy to find. We can help by building and offering the owls shelter and a place to rear their young in the form of expertly placed owl boxes. It's the least we can do for the Barn Owls for providing us with such beauty and inspiration for generations.

Robin
in a Holly Bush
Erithacus rubecula

Feeling Christmassy yet? The sight of a
puffered-up Robin in a holly bush can make
even the most Scrooge-like duck smile a
little. The holly is a vivacious bush that grows
everywhere all year round – woods, parks,
gardens and hedgerows are bursting with this
prickly Yuletide icon. Their glossy, spiky
leaves and the fruit's toxicity keeps us at bay,
but during winter when the berries shine
bright red it makes a perfect salvation for any
hungry, cold bird needing to stock
up for Christmas.

SPOTTING AND JOTTING

It's great spotting a bird you've never seen before, so here's a handy way of keeping all your jottings in check. Get spotting either by sitting comfortably at your window, or pull on some boots, grab a flask and binoculars, and go outside. Happy spotting!

☐ Bullfinches

☐ Goldfinches

☐ Crested Tit

☐ Long-tailed Tit

☐ Hobby

☐ Merlin

☐ Common Buzzard

☐ Goshawk

☐ Nuthatch

☐ Treecreeper

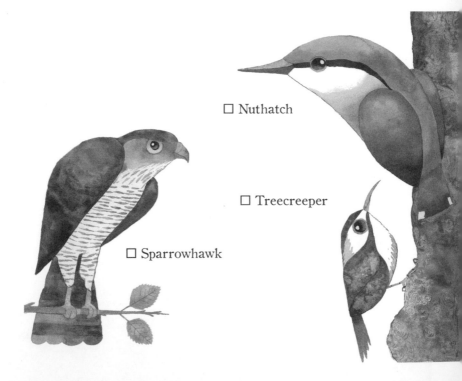

☐ Sparrowhawk

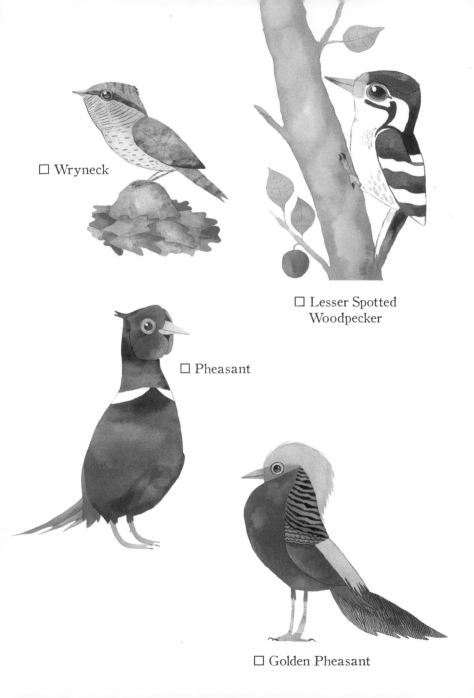

☐ Wryneck

☐ Lesser Spotted
Woodpecker

☐ Pheasant

☐ Golden Pheasant

☐ Black Grouse

☐ Goldeneye

☐ Moorhen

☐ Woodcock

☐ Serin

☐ Whinchat

☐ Cirl Bunting

☐ Woodlark

☐ Bluethroat

☐ Tree Pipit

☐ Black Redstart

☐ Ring Ouzel

☐ Fieldfare

☐ Waxwings

☐ Spotted Flycatcher

☐ A Parliament of Young Tawny Owls

☐ European Eagle Owl

□ Red-backed Shrike

□ Great Grey Shrike

□ Jay

□ Nutcracker

 ☐ Jackdaw

 ☐ A Rookery

☐ Hooded Crow

 ☐ A Tidings
of Magpies

☐ Blue Tit

☐ Redpoll

☐ Golden Oriole

☐ Ring-necked
   Parakeet

☐ Stock Dove

☐ Blackcaps

□ A Siege
  of Herons

□ Barn Owl
  Nest Box

□ Robin

ACKNOWLEDGEMENTS

Thank you to:

The Goldfinches, The Sewells, The Roses
and The Lees.

Edwyn and Grace, Simon Benham, Jeff, Robin,
Andrew and all at Caught By The River.

Phil Aylen's *Owls* and the 1981 edition of
the *Reader's Digest Field Guide to the
Birds of Britain* - my bible since I was 8.

Untold gratitude to all the woods I've ever walked
in and to all the birds that have come and said hi.

Find out more about Matt and his work at
www.mattsewell.co.uk